Beautiful Caves
For Kids!

Nature Books for Kids
By
K. Bennett

JD-Biz Publishing

Read More Amazing Animal Books

Purchase at Amazon.com

Table of Contents

Introduction

*Look deep into nature, and then you will understand everything better~ **Albert Einstein***

***

Caves: Do you like to explore and learn about new things? I do! What about your imagination? Do you like to use it? If you do, think about this for a moment:

Imagine you are walking or playing outside one day. It's nice and sunny, the breeze is blowing, the flowers are bright and colorful and the grass smells fresh and green.

A beautiful butterfly flitters by with multicolored wings. You decide to chase it and before you know what is happening, you get deeper and deeper into the woods. Are you afraid? No way! You are an explorer and an explorer is very brave.

The butterfly disappears and you find yourself in a place with large trees high above your head. They have huge roots, big enough for you to sleep on and bright green leaves.

When you step closer into this strange world, funny plants gently brush your leg. It's like they are saying: *Hello! Where did you come from?*

You walk a little more and suddenly, you find a large hole in the ground. Or it might be a gap instead of a hole, or an opening of some kind. What is it? Yes! It's a Cave. What a great discovery for a brave explorer!

You stare inside curiously but guess what? You can't see a thing! It's much too dark in there. Do you still feel like exploring or do you want to go back home?

If you are just a little bit adventurous, you might want to find out what's inside. Do you want to try? Tell you what… I will go with you and together we will explore the Cave and see what wonders we can discover. Are you ready? Then, let's do it!

Journey to the ends of the Earth

Before we start to explore, we need to take some important things with us. Do you remember how dark the Cave is? Can you guess what we need to find our way around? Did you guess light? Very good!

Many Caves are cold or very cool so we will need to get some warm clothes to put on. Do you want to know how cool they can get?

Mammoth Cave is a beautiful cave in the National Park of Kentucky, USA. This cave can be 54 degrees all year round but sometimes it can even get cooler depending on the wind. So if you wanted to visit this Cave, you will need a 'sweater or jacket.'

Of course not all caves are cool. Some Caves like those on Hawaii Island can be too hot to visit! But today, let's explore a Cave that is cool and not too warm.

All right Explorer, what do we have so far? Did you guess light and warm clothes? Great job!

What else do we need?

We will be doing a lot of walking so you need good shoes. What kind of shoes do you think is best for walking in a cave?

Sandals? High heels? Sneakers? Hiking boots?

Which one will you choose?

Did you choose hiking boots? Awesome!

Why do you need hiking boots? Many caves are wet and this can make them slippery. Hiking boots have good traction that will help your feet to keep steady while you walk. So if you want to be comfortable as you explore, hiking boots are a great choice.

If you don't like the idea of hiking boots, you can wear something else but your shoes should have these three important things:

1-watertight: (This means no water should be able to get inside your shoe)

2-Stiff sole: (This will help your foot to stand without slipping and sliding all over the place!)

3-Durable: (Your shoe should last for the whole trip and not break apart halfway! Then you would be barefoot and that is not a good idea, right?)

Source: http://outdoors.stackexchange.com/

Ok! We have light, clothes and shoes? Great! Can you think of anything else to add to this list?

What about a notebook? You might want to write down some of the amazing things we will see. How about a Camera to take beautiful pictures and maybe a snack or two? What about water to keep you well hydrated? These are great choices!

Do you think you're ready? Wonderful!

Enjoy your adventure and don't forget to share your findings with others!

DID YOU KNOW?

Many people love to explore caves as a hobby! This is called *SPELUNKING*. Have you ever heard the word before? Wikihow has an excellent 5 step process on the best way to go Spelunking. Here are the tips!

Step 1: ***Don't go alone.*** Always travel with a group. You never know when you might have an emergency or need help!

Step 2: ***Have the right equipment.*** Just like a chef needs the right ingredients to make at tasty meal, a caver needs the right equipment!

Step 3: *Know where you're going*. Caves have lots of twists and turns, so leave clues to find you way back!

Step 4: *You are on your own*. Caves can change quickly and if you don't know what you are doing, you may get hurt.

Step 5: *Leave only memories behind.* Don't change the cave or add anything to it. Have you heard of this saying: "Leave nothing but footprints, take nothing but memories?"

And finally, have fun!

(Source: http://www.wikihow.com/Go-Caving-(Spelunking)

COOL FACTS FOR KIDS:

One of the best caves for families and young ones to visit is *Cave of the Winds* in Colorado. They offer 3 tours and exciting adventures on each one. You can choose the Discovery tour, the Lantern tour or the Caving 101 tour.

The Discovery tour is a great for families. It is only 45 minutes but you get to see amazing sites like the Temple of Silence or the Bridal Chamber!

You even get to spend a little time to total darkness to see what it feels like. If you are even more adventurous you might choose to try the *"Wind Walker Challenge Course."*

This is a 3 obstacle course with a maze of steel beams, swinging ropes and ladders along the edge of a very large drop. If you love excitement and adventure this might be perfect for you.

Go online to find out more, but don't forget to get permission before you search!

(Source: http://caveofthewinds.com/)

Chapter 1

Let's Explore!

Ok Explorer! Let's find out what Caves are all about and then we will choose which one we want to explore!

What is a Cave?

Answer: Sciencekids.co.nz defines Caves like this:

"A cave (or cavern) is a naturally occurring area or space under the surface of the Earth. Caves are often a system of interconnected passageways created by the weathering of rock."

Do you understand what this means? To begin with, Caves are a natural part of Planet Earth just like the mountains. The interesting thing about Caves is how complicated they can get! For example, a Cave can have lots of different passages. Think of it has a highway with lots of different lanes going everywhere!

Unlike a highway, Caves are made up of rocks and other formations that we will talk about later. This makes Caves one of a kind! Let's see why.

Different types of Caves

The National Caves Association lists many different types of Caves.

Solutional Cave

These types of cave have soluble or soft rocks like Limestone but there are other types of rocks too like: Marble, salt, gypsum and dolomite.

Primary Cave

A Cave that is formed at the same time as the rock around it is called a Primary Cave. A lava tube is an example you can think about. For example, let's say a Volcano erupts and a tube of Lava flows down a hill. When it cools down and gets really hard, the inside of the Lava tube is hollow and this is where a Cave forms!

Sea Cave

This one is my favorite. These types of Caves can be found in many places around the world. They are on the coastline and very beautiful. But they can also be dangerous. Can you guess what's inside a Sea Cave? Did you guess lots of water? Very good!

Glacier Cave

These types of Caves are very unique. They are formed by melting ice and water. As the years go by, these Caves change when the ice melts and the water flows around them. Sometimes they even fall in on themselves! I do not think I want to be inside when this happens... do you?

(*Source:* *http://www.cavern.com/Learn/cavetypes.asp*)

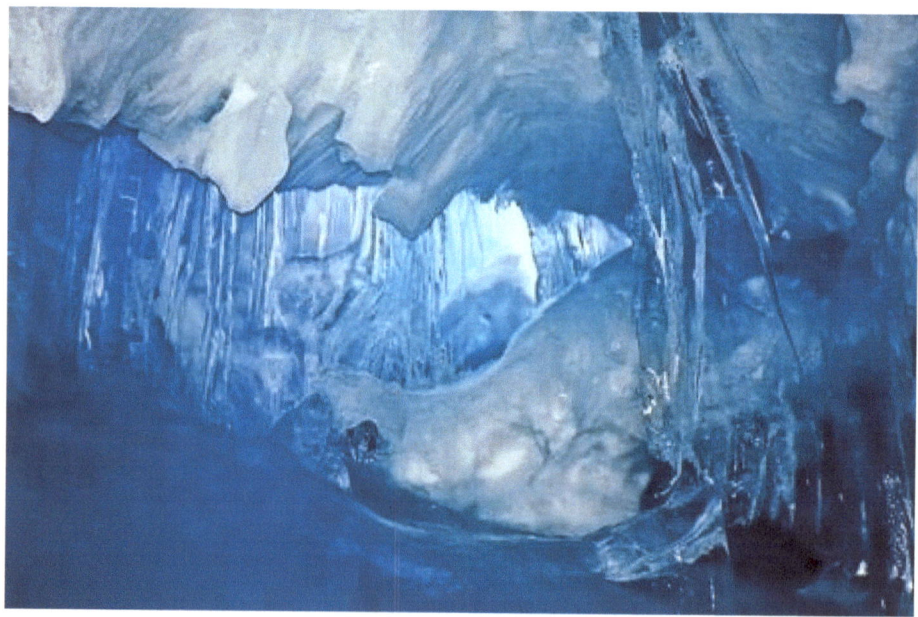

There are many other types of Caves on the planet, so I invite you to explore and see what else you can find! Don't forget to ask your parent or a guardian's permission before you search!

How are Caves formed?

Caves have a very interesting life! Did you know they take a long time to form? Can you guess how many years it takes a Cave to become a Cave?

Hundreds? Thousands? Millions?

Pick a number…

Many scientists say it took *millions* of years! Do you want to know how a Cave becomes a Cave?

They usually start out as simple rock formations. Then when some years go by they change and get more rock formations. And after many more years of changes they slowly turn into a Cave. As you can see, it takes a very long time!

Why are Caves so special?

One of the most important reasons why Caves are so special is because of the things we find inside. Do you have your light, clothes and boots ready?

If you do… and if you are ready to explore, come with me and let's see what kinds of things we can discover in this Cave!

FUN FACTS FOR KIDS:

In the Utah Valley, Utah…there is a very interesting Cave called **Blowhole**. What makes this Cave very special is the wall. It's called an "Indian Blanket." Do you know why? Ask your parent or a guardian to help you search. Then after you find the answer, share your findings with others.

Remember: Sharing your ideas is a great way to make friends!

All right, now that you are ready to explore the cave, use your flashlight and tell me what you see…

Caves have unique formations all over the place! These formations have interesting names like: Stalactites, stalagmites, helictites, and several more.

Do these names sound funny to you? Let's learn a little bit about them!

-Stalactites: These look like icicles hanging from the ceiling but they are not made of ice! They are formed by mineral deposits which get hard over time. Kind of like water in the freezer that gets hard after a while!

-Stalagmites: Instead of hanging from the ceiling, these formations come up from the ground. Be careful and watch where you put your foot!

-Helictites: You can find these formations on the walls or the ceilings. Some of them look a lot like spaghetti strings, but don't try to eat them! These formations are caused by water and calcite deposits from the water pressure.

-Curtains: Some of them look like hard strips of bacon and others look like icicles. But I do not think you should try to eat or lick them! Curtains are made of mineral and they are folded on top of each other like huge sheets. They are not thick but very thin.

- Cave Pearls: These sound very pretty and guess what? They are! Do you know how a pearl is made in the sea? Cave Pearls are a lot like this. After years and years of calcite deposits covering grains of sand or dirt, these pearls are formed. And they look a lot like Oyster pearls! Maybe we will see some Cave Pearls on our exploration. What do you think?

-Column: This formation is very easy to see. This happens with a Stalactite and a Stalagmite grows so close to each other that they touch and form a Column! Then they both keep growing as one formation instead of two. Pretty neat!

-Draperies: Do draperies and curtains sound the same? You are right! They are also known as curtains. These formations happen when water runs down the walls of the cave and calcite gets all over the place. Sometimes you will find draperies hanging from the ceilings or at the end of other formations!

-Shelfstone: You will find these types of formations around cave pools. They will tell you if cave pools used to be there! It will also show you how high or low the water used to get. These formations can be thin or very thick. Can you see them?

-Pool Spar: And here we find more water formations! This happens when water has been in the Cave for a very long time. This calcite or gypsum crystallizes and forms a very pretty crystal!

Now that you know the different formations, can you remember them all? If you do, there is a way you can keep them in mind. Cave formations are called by only ONE name. Can you guess which name it might be?

I will tell you at the end of the book!

(Source: http://www.hometrainingtools.com/a/stalactites-stalagmites-science-teaching-tip)

(Source: http://www.caverntours.com/KIDSPAGE_Formations.html)

TEST YOUR RESEARCH SKILLS!

Guess the name and find the Cave...

To visit this cave you need to be at least 42 inches tall! How tall are you?

The tour lasts for 90 minutes and you get to see some fascinating formations on the tour. But if you have heart or breathing problems, this tour is not recommended! Why?

At one part of the Cave you need to climb 500 stairs! When you are at the end of the climb you will be around 230 feet in the air.

Can you guess where this Cave is? Do some research and find out but don't forget to get permission BEFORE you search.

Have fun!

Chapter 2

Caves are Amazing!

Now that you know what kinds of formations you will find in Caves, let's learn about four types of Caves around the world and what makes them special!

Winter Ice Caves - Iceland

This type of Cave tour is for the brave! Why? Do you remember what can happen to a Glacier Cave? Yes, they can collapse and fall on top of you!

If you decide to tour a Glacier Cave, you need to be very careful and you need a guide to show you the way. Never go by yourself!

Can you guess why a guide is very important on this type of tour? They not only show you where to go, but they test the Cave as you explore. They want to make sure you will always be safe.

Winter Ice Caves are beautiful and you will see lots and lots of ice formations in beautiful designs.

1- Mammoth Cave

This cave is found in the National Park of Kentucky. One special attraction in this Cave is the **Frozen Niagara Tour**. This is the perfect tour for small children or older ones who have trouble walking. It is just a short tour but you get to see exciting formations on the Cave walls.

If you prefer a more dramatic tour with lots of pits, domes and passageways you might prefer the **Domes and Dripstone Tours**. You get to see the Niagara Tour on this expedition as well. Which one do you prefer?

2- Eisriesenwelt Cave - Austria

This cave is a very special Cave found in the Alps of Austria. Do you know why this Cave is so special? It is full of beautiful ice formations that melt during summer and freeze during winter! It is also the largest Ice Cave in the world and is 26 miles long. Would you like to visit this Cave?

3- *Cave of Crystals - Mexico*

If you want to see big, beautiful crystals this is the cave for you. The largest crystal they discovered is 36 feet long and weighs 55 tons! That's a very big crystal.

FUN FACTS FOR KIDS:

Glacier Caves and Ice Caves may seem a lot alike but they are two different things. What makes them so different?

A Glacier Cave forms when the ice melts and starts to run through the Glacier. If the water is warm enough it makes an opening or a Cave.

In summer, the Glacier may melt some more and soon you will have a nice big Cave to explore. Summer is not the only reason warm water runs through a Glacier. Think about underwater Volcanoes geothermal vents of warm water. All of these can make a big hole in the Glacier to form a Cave!

How are Ice Caves different? Ice Caves have ice all year round. It does not need to wait for warm water to run through it to form a Cave. Ice Caves are very cold and some parts of it fall to 32°F. Brrrrrrr!!!

Chapter 3

More Fun facts!

Did you have fun learning about different types of Caves? Great! What else can we learn about them?

- Cave formations are not the only things you find in Caves. Many creatures live there too! Creatures like: Bats, Bears, Spiders, crickets, Earthworms, Salamanders and even fish! Some of the creatures are called Cave dwellers because they look different than normal creatures. Some of them have no color and many are blind.

-Caves are also full of pictures! Did you know Cave paintings are found in every continent around the world except for Antarctica? No one really knows where most came from but they are pretty to look at. Lots of animals are on the Cave walls like horses, bulls, deer's, giraffes, Rhinoceros and many others!

-There are many Caves around the world but no one really knows how many there are. Some say there are millions of them all over the planet. That's a lot of Caves!

-In New Zealand there is a very interesting Cave with lots of light called Waitomo Caves. The creatures that live in this Cave are beautiful glowworms about the size of a mosquito! They may be very small but they have a big, bright light and are very famous. Did you know these small creatures are only found in New Zealand?

-The Mulu Caves of Malaysia are very big Caves with large chambers! Some say you can fit many airplanes inside the Sarawak Chamber. How many? Over 40! Wow!!! That's a very big chamber!

-If you want to explore a Cave or make it a hobby this is called: Spelunking or Caving!

-If you want to study Caves you need to become a Speleologist!

(Source: http://www.kidsdiscover.com/spotlight/caves-for-kids/ & http://www.touropia.com/famous-underground-caves-in-the-world/)

Conclusion:

In conclusion: Learning about Caves can be lots of fun! Would you like to continue learning a little more about them? Then let me give you the answer to the question I posed in Chapter 1. The name of the formations found in caves is: ***Speleothems.*** Did you guess the word?

*Here are some more ideas to help you in your Spelunking quest!

Choose a Cave you would like to learn about and answer the following questions:

-When was it discovered?

-How big is it?

-Can you explore on your own or do you need a guide?

-Where is it located?

-What is the temperature?

-What are the good things about the Cave?

-What are the bad things about the Cave?

-What kind of equipment do you need to explore?

-What kind of clothes do you need to wear?

-Is it great for children and older ones or only for adults in good physical health?

Test your theories and come up with a conclusion!

Another creative idea for you!

Pick a Cave, any Cave. Imagine you get lost inside. How will you survive? What can you do for food and water? How long will it take you to find your way out?

Then decide:

What supplies do I need? What supplies don't I need? Where can I find water? If there is no water, what else can I do? What skills do I need?

What other questions can you think of? I am sure you have much better ideas! So put on your thinking cap and come up with your own conclusions.

I hope you enjoyed this book on **Beautiful Caves** and always remember…

"Educating the mind without educating the heart is no education at all." - *Aristotle*

Happy reading!

Author Bio

K. Bennett loves to write for both children and adults. Many different subjects are interesting to develop, but writing for children is special to her heart.

Her favorite pastimes include reading, traveling and discovering new things. Each of these activities helps to fuel her imagination and acts like a blank canvas waiting for more stories.

She is intrigued with fantasy elements like hidden worlds and faraway lands. And basically anything that gets her imagination soaring to new heights!

Her writing credits include children books online and other writing works listed at Amazon.com.

Our books are available at:

1. Amazon.com

2. Barnes and Noble

3. Itunes

4. Kobo

5. Smashwords

6. Google Play Books

Publisher

JD-Biz Corp

P O Box 374

Mendon, Utah 84325

http://www.jd-biz.com/

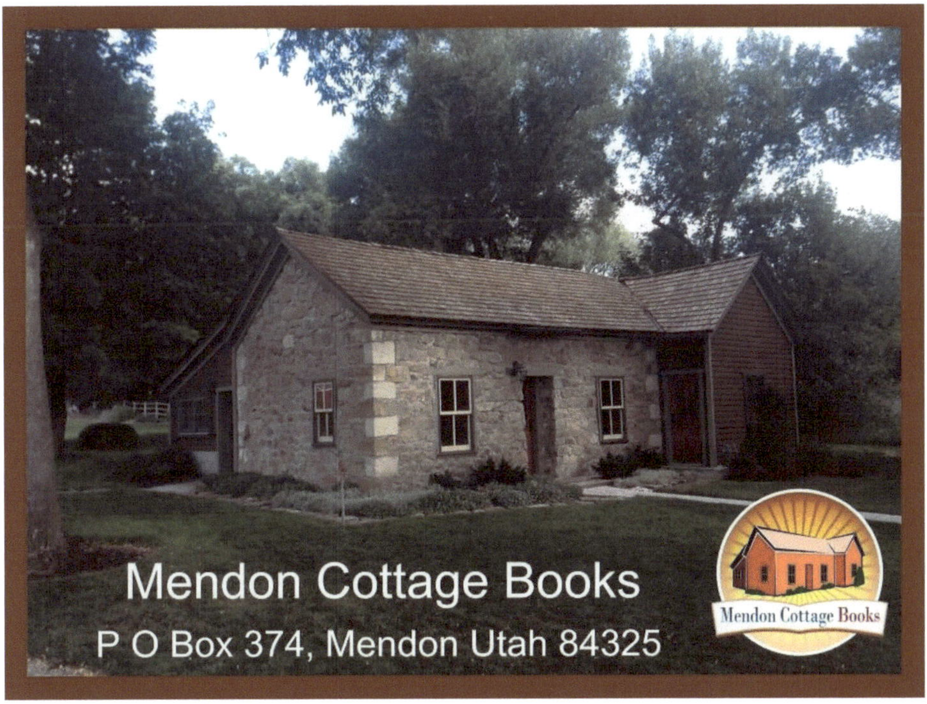

Mendon Cottage Books

P O Box 374, Mendon Utah 84325

Horses
For Kids
Amazing Animal Books
For Young Readers
By John and
Annalee Davidson

Ponies
For Kids
Amazing Animal Books
For Young Readers
Rachel Smith

Ten Amazing Horses For Kids
Nature Books for Kids
JD-Biz Publishing
K. Bennett

Akhal-Teke "The Golden Horse of the desert" For Kids
Nature Books for Kids
JD-Biz Publishing
K. Bennett

Suffolk-Punch "The Gentle Giant" For Kids
Nature Books for Kids
JD-Biz Publishing
K. Bennett

Shires "The great Horse" For Kids
Nature Books for Kids
JD-Biz Publishing
K. Bennett

Colonial Spanish "Horse of the Americas" For Kids
Nature Books for Kids
JD-Biz Publishing
K. Bennett

Canadian "The Little Iron Horse" For Kids
Nature Books for Kids
JD-Biz Publishing
K. Bennett

Cleveland Bays "History and Future" Horses For Kids
Nature Books for Kids
JD-Biz Publishing
K. Bennett

Dinosaurs For Kids	**Ankylosaurus** The Armored Dinosaur	**Tyrannosaurus Rex** For Kids	**Apatosaurus** The Thunder Lizard	**Archaeopteryx** Ancient Wings
Smilodon Saber-toothed Tiger	**Pterosaurs** The Flying Reptiles	**Dilophosaurus** The Two-Crested Dinosaur	**Introduction to Dinosaurs**	**Allosaurus** The Strange Reptile
Dimetrodon Permian Predator	**Triceratops** The Three-Horned Dinosaur	**Spinosaurus** The Spine Reptile	**Megalodon** The Mega Shark!	**Pachycephalosaurus** Thick-Headed Lizard
Parasaurolophus The Crested Reptile	**Sarcosuchus** King Crocodile	**Stegosaurus** The Dinosaur with a Roof	**Troodon** The Wounding Tooth	**Tylosaurus** Predator of the Deep
Crocodiles For Kids	**Carnataurus** The Horned Predator	**Salamanders** For Kids	**Crocodilians** For Kids	**Lizards** For Kids

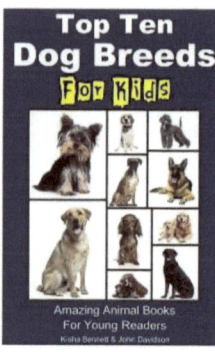

Top Ten Dog Breeds For Kids

Amazing Animal Books For Young Readers
Kisha Beratell & John Davidson

German Shepherds

Dog Books for Kids
K. Bennett

Bulldogs

Dog Books for Kids
K. Bennett

Dachshund

Dog Books for Kids
K. Bennett

Poodles

Dog Books for Kids
K. Bennett

Labrador Retrievers

Dog Books for Kids
K. Bennett

Rottweilers

Dog Books for Kids
K. Bennett

Boxers

Dog Books for Kids
K. Bennett

Golden Retrievers

Dog Books for Kids
K. Bennett

Puppies

Dog Books For Kids

Amazing Animal Books
By John Davidson

Beagles

Dog Books for Kids
K. Bennett

Yorkshire Terriers

Dog Books for Kids
K. Bennett

Dogs
Top Ten Dog Breeds For Kids

Amazing Animal Books For Young Readers
Zahra Jazeel & John Davidson

Cats For Kids

Amazing Animal Books For Young Readers
K. Bennett & John Davidson

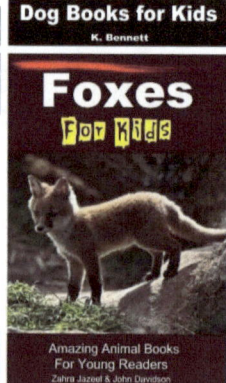

Foxes For Kids

Amazing Animal Books For Young Readers
Zahra Jazeel & John Davidson

Wolves For Kids

Amazing Animal Books For Young Readers
By John Davidson and Virginia Fidler

www.ingramcontent.com/pod-product-compliance
Lightning Source LLC
Chambersburg PA
CBHW050844290526
45792CB00002B/511